LEARN HOW TO BECOME A BLOGGER.

An EASY step-by-step guide to
starting your own blog

w. www.start-flourishing.com
e. contact@start-flourishing.com

Dedication
To Sam, for sharing your knowledge.

LEARN HOW TO BECOME A BLOGGER.

An EASY step-by-step guide to
starting your own blog

Contents

GENERAL INTRODUCTION

Have you ever thought about starting a blog? Well now you can!

I wanted to create this book as I not only love the subject, but I love to help people who have ambition. I have been a web developer for a number of years, and, at the start of 2018 I developed and launched my own personal blog (www.start-flourishing.com). Here, I provide advice on how to take control of your own personal finances, how to increase your personal wealth with additional income resources, and how to get started in the wider world of investing.

In this guide, learning how to become a blogger is broken down into easily manageable chapters. The aim is to provide you with an easy step-by-step guide on the process: from setting up your own blog, all the way through to maintaining it. Throughout, you will find exercises to help get that creativity flowing through you. At the end of each section, you will also find a checklist to help you tick off all the important steps, so you too can launch a blog that you can be really proud of.

Becoming a successful blogger takes a tremendous amount of time and effort. As you progress through this book, you will come to experience this too. However, the beauty of blogging is that you have the opportunity to learn such a vast range of skills; there is so much to discover. You can develop skills in viable careers such as writing, designing, photography, marketing, social media managing, and PR - who knows what opportunities this could open for you.

Even though this book is designed for absolute beginners, if you are already a seasoned blogger I am sure you will find some parts useful, especially the chapters on website maintenance and generating traffic.

Who is this book for?

- Those that would you like to learn something new
- Are passionate about writing and sharing knowledge
- Connecting with like-minded people
- Enjoy being creative
- Know how to use the internet
- Have frequent access to a computer
- Importantly, those that have no idea on how to start blogging

You probably don't need to read this book if...

- You are already a seasoned blogger with thousands of followers, although you may still learn something new
- Not prepared to put in hard work
- Afraid to try something new
- Don't know how to turn on a computer

INTRODUCTION

The history of blogging

The term blog, first known as a weblog, dates back to 1997. Historians often attribute the creation of the term 'weblog' to Jorn Barger, a frequent blogger himself. It was then in 1999 that programmer Peter Merholz shortened the term to the more commonly used word: 'blog'. It is generally acknowledged, however, that blogs existed as early as 1994 but were simply referred to as personal homepages instead. Part of this stems from the main use of blogs in this period. Most resembled online diaries where users would chronicle the events of their day to share with a wider audience.

After a slower than expected start, by the turn of the century blogging quickly grew in popularity. The first hosted blog tools helped spur this growth. Websites such as 'Open Diary', 'SlashDot', and 'Blogger.com' introduced common blog components today such as a comments section and syndication platforms. The growth in search engines helped spur the boom further as it was now increasingly easier to access a wide variety of blogs without having to manually scour through them for content.

From 2004, blogs began to grow even more mainstream. News services, political candidates, and political consultants began utilizing blogs to help others understand their way of thinking and to reach out to new potential customers/ voters. At this point, blogs became an almost mandatory tool for politics. In 2004, Merriam-Webster's Dictionary further declared 'blog' their word of the year.

Today, there are few people out there that have not heard of the term 'blog'. Experts estimate that there are approximately 152 million blogs out there right now. However, the number of them that remain active is harder to calculate. Sadly, some are neglected after a mere few hours, but others thrive for years, if not decades.

What exactly is a blog and why are they popular?

The Oxford English Dictionary defines a blog as a 'frequently updated website, typically run by a single person and consisting of personal observations arranged in chronological order, with excerpts from other sources, hyperlinks to other sites, etc.' Today, however, there is a far broader range of blogs than those created by a single person. Blogs are frequently used for a wide variety of purposes.

Though blogs started as persona diaries, today personal blogs also focus on hobbies, interests, causes, or whatever is happening in one's life at the time. Personal blogs have also taken on a new dynamic known as 'vlogs'. Moving away from the traditional written side of blogging, some users share their lives in video blog ('vlog') format.

Business blogs have also been growing in popularity. The ultimate aim of these blogs is to gain greater traffic, exposure, and ultimately/ most obviously, business. Lately the internet has also seen a rise in affiliate bloggers who gain money based on commission. The goal is to encourage visitors to buy the products they have displayed in their posts.

The important thing to highlight is that there is no specific 'one-size-fits-all' type of blogger. Many people blog, and for a wide variety of reasons too.

Reasons to start a blog

1. A new hobby/ learning new skills
There's never a better time than now to start a new hobby. Be sure to set yourself goals to help you stay on track and remain motivated. As we have seen, not all blogs are just hobbies, some are for professional purposes, but

7

if you wish to blog for pleasure, it can be a very rewarding and fulfilling experience.

Blogging also provides an opportunity to learn a plethora of new skills. It is likely that as your blog builds you may have to dabble in HTML and CSS coding. While it is not essential, and sometimes bloggers pay others to do this for them, it is a very good way to learn new tech-related skills. Another example comes from digital marketing. Those heavily involved in blogging often end up learning more about advertising themselves online as well as the highs and lows of social networks such as Facebook, Instagram, Twitter and Pinterest.

2. Tell your story and help to inspire others

Many people use their blogs to tell their story and inspire others. This can be in a variety of ways and to a multitude of ends. For example, some enjoy sharing tales from their travels in order to inspire others to visit the locations they have enjoyed. Alternatively, others may share their experiences with different illnesses, from cancer to Parkinson's disease or depression. Sharing these experiences can help others suffering from similar conditions or help generally raise awareness of the illness itself and hope people grow to understand it better.

3. Become a better writer and thinker

As a blogger, instant feedback will allow you to monitor how you are doing. Programs that track visitors to your site will allow you to see how successful your work is. If your work is good, you should get positive responses that follow. Otherwise, negative feedback or none at all will let you know that you may need to improve your style of writing. This gives you the opportunity to explore various methods to see what works best for you. Further, blogs allow you to expand as a thinker as they provide an ideal platform to experiment with new ideas and forms of writing.

4. Meet new people on the same wavelength as you

Blogging provides a great opportunity to find people who share the same interests and hobbies as you. I know certain types of blogs have a whole network of bloggers sharing ideas behind them. On Facebook, for example, over three-thousand users have joined a platform called 'Female Travel Bloggers' to share tips and hints on how to succeed and ask the community questions. People that take the time to read your posts undoubtedly have an interest in what you are doing, and it can be fun to share your experiences with them and bounce ideas around.

5. It can help to grow your business

Blogging can help you grow your business in a variety of ways. Most importantly, blogging can help you to attract new customers. To do this you must ensure your articles are easily accessible online, look up search engine optimization for more information on this. Ultimately though, your blog posts must be compelling enough to encourage customers to purchase your products. You can also use your blog to address issues your customers have raised and to highlight how you plan on improving the situation. This lets customers know you are open to change and welcome ways to improve.

Blogging can also help you to establish yourself as an expert in your field as you get to share your knowledge with the world. This makes your business appear more helpful and creates brand-awareness. Finally, blogging can also help to attract business relationships too as referrals from other business may help yours grow as well.

6. Make money

Blogs can be a very profitable form of income if done correctly. It all starts with generating useful content and finding readers that are willing to engage with it. From here, there are several ways to monetize your blog. Affiliate marketing is just one way we have already looked at. You can also offer products on your blog, both virtual (e.g. eBooks, courses, software, apps etc.) and physical (merchandise, teaching material, books etc.). Many bloggers also make money from advertising on their blog. This can be in the form of sponsored posts, ambassadorships, text links, competitions and giveaways, and ad networks such as Google Ads.

Other forms of blog income that are often forgotten about include recurring revenue. This is where readers pay regular sums of money to access items such as premium content subscriptions, online coaching, and private communities. Blogs also offer a good way to market your services: from freelancing to consulting to designing and copywriting, blogs offer the opportunity to showcase all these skills.

7. It's free

Ok, well, most of the time. It really is as easy as hitting go. Of course, it really depends on the type of blog you want to create. If it is a personal blog then platforms such as blogger, WordPress, and Squarespace offer easy-to-use templates for free. If you want to customize these templates further, or use a custom domain name, then many websites do charge additional fees, particularly if you are opening a business blog.

PLANNING

Any big project that you decide to start should require careful planning. Planning provides guidance, organization and direction. Without it you'd just be aimlessly wondering what to do or forever changing your mind.

Give the planning phase of your blog your utmost attention. Consider writing a business plan as this will help you set up and formulate a strategy by presenting a step by step guide to grow your blog. Don't worry, it doesn't have to be a formal document. But create something that you can refer to when making decisions and review it periodically, as it does not have to be set in stone.

Let's delve deeper into each of the planning stages of starting a blog.

What to blog about?

So, would like to start a blog, but now you have no idea what topic to actually write about. What's next? The key thing here is to consider what your goal is with your blog. If it is to meet like-minded people, then blog about something you love and enjoy writing about. If it is to become a better writer, then why not choose a niche topic and attempt to excel in your chosen field. Overall, if you are writing for fun just make sure it is something you are passionate about! It is very hard otherwise to continue creating engaging content.

Of course, if your blog is related to your business, then choosing what to blog about really depends on the products you intend on selling. Think about your blog as a marketing channel, just like email marketing, direct mail, or social media, you can use it to support business growth. Consequently, think about what your customer would like to see. If you are a car parts supplier, why not write about additional car parts that would make their car really wow a crowd? If you are a bank, why not write some posts including a more detailed description of the services you offer? Or advice on how to re-mortgage? There are a whole variety of fun and different ways to stand out.

♀ Tip:

Take a look at other blogs with similar interests to your topic and see how you could do it differently. How could you make it better? What other information could you add to provide a solution to readers problems?

✏ Grab a pen:

Write down 10 ideas on what you could start blogging about. What really inspires or motivates you? What information could you pass on to others? Do you have a very specific niche or hobby that people might find interesting?

1.

2.

3.

4.

5.

6.

7.

8.

9.

10.

How to choose a name for your blog?

Choosing a name for your blog often seems like a really daunting task. There are so many blogs out there that is hard to distinguish yourself. A blog name can really make or break your success! Choose carefully.

As a starting point, it is a good idea to write down the topics you plan on blogging about. This will enable you to really incorporate your main theme into your blog title. It is also advisable to explore similar blogs to grasp what is out there already; you do not want to pick something and find that another company or person already has the exact same name.

You should also consider the audience you are writing for. Think about what you would google to find a blog like yours. This will also help you later when it comes to optimizing your blog for search engines. Remember, you also need a blog name that is easy to both pronounce and spell. This will increase the chances of people both remembering and finding your blog.

Once you have narrowed your names down to a short list, it is a smart idea to check these ideas against a domain name website such as GoDaddy. This will show you if the blog name you desire is already in use, and how much it would be to purchase this domain name (e.g. www.iloveblogging.com) if you wanted it later down the line. If all else fails and you really cannot decide from your shortened list, why not ask your friends? Alternatively, if you are feeling bold, just flip a coin and hope you make your mind up the second the answer is revealed!

Clarify your content strategy

Content strategy, as defined by Kristina Halvorson, is the "creation, publication, and governance of useful, usable content." Consequently, content strategy refers to the overall plan for your blog. It is important to bare this in mind throughout the process of establishing and up-keeping your blog. Content marketing refers to the vision, goals, voice, style and publication of your blog and so the two greatly overlap.

When it comes to strategy, it is important to consider the following questions: Who are you creating content for? Who will be your audience? What formats do you intend to focus on? Where will you publish your work? How will it be unique? What keywords will you use? How will you develop ideas for subjects over time?

Firstly, it is essential to outline your goals before you start your blog. Use SMART goals – specific, measurable, attainable, relevant, and time-orientated. Setting goals, especially ones with times in mind, gives you something to work towards and ensure you are on-track. It's a good idea to set out both long-term and short-term goals – think yearly, monthly, weekly, and daily. Be sure to keep them realistic as an overly-ambitious plan can lead you to grow disheartened quickly.

When writing your goals, you need to consider who will be your audience, thus what they may like to read. If you understand who your target audience is, you will be able to produce more valuable and relevant content that they will want to engage with. After you have established this, you should then brainstorm ideas for content. It can be a good idea to turn to social media to see what is performing well already, or what you believe is missing from the market as this can help inspire new ideas. In doing so, consider how you are to develop ideas for subjects over time, and all the ways to do so.

In order to see if you are meeting your goals, it is advisable to have success metrics defined for each post. To begin with, consider traffic to each post, engagement metrics (i.e. number of pages visited, time on page etc.), and how many social shares the post garnered. You can then use this data to assess if there are any patterns and where gaps lie. It will help you develop your strategy as you progress.

> ## ♀ Tip:
>
> **Google analytics offers a great insight in finding out how many visitors are coming to your blog, and which pages are being clicked the most. Plus, it's completely free! More on that later.**

Now you have established both your audience and content, you need to think about how often you are going to post on your blog. How much time do you want to dedicate to your pursuit? Are you going to publish daily at a certain time? Can readers expect an update every Wednesday at 7pm? Knowing when and how often you will post can improve how your blog performs as consistency allows people to know when to expect new content and attracts new readers.

Finally, marketing your content is obviously very important. Search engine optimization (SEO) is one of the most popular focuses of marketing today. SEO aims to improve organic (non-paid) search engine results (from websites such as Google and Yahoo) in order to improve your ranking thus making your blog easier to find and drive more traffic to it.

There are many components to SEO as search engines do not make public the criteria for ranking top of a search. However, experts believe it is a combination of things including how easy your website is navigate and use, how quickly you provide direct information to a query, how compatible with browsers your website is, and the quality and creditability of the content you produce (to name a few).

A lot of these aspects will be explored later on. Another that is important to mention is keyword research because this is one of the most high-return and valuable activities in the SEO department. Conducting keyword research will ensure you rank for appropriate topics. Do not think solely about getting people to visit your site, rather the type of people you are hoping to attract as this will ensure they are repeat visitors. There are several keyword research tools out there, such as Google AdWords, that can help in this task and determine the value of each keyword. Again, this will be explored in greater depth shortly.

Now you have done all this, what's next?

Decide on your blogging platform

Today, there are many different blogging platforms that provide a variety of different services. With each, however, you need to consider how flexible you want your website to be. Do you want an easy-to-use ready-made platform? Or do you want your own domain name and a more personalized website? Some of the more popular blogging platforms include: Wordpress. org, Wordpress.com, Joomla, Drupal, Magento, Squarespace, Blogger, Tumblr, Wix etc.

Read on to find out the advantages and disadvantages of different types of blogging platforms. WordPress.org will be used as the example blogging platform throughout this book. As of 2017, 26.9% of all websites on the web now use WordPress as their content management system.

Which of the following platforms do you recognize? Try and match the name to the logo.

WiX.com

Medium

WordPress

Drupal

Joomla

Wix

Blogger

Squarespace

tumblr

Option 1 - A free blogging platform (wordpress.com)

<u>Pros</u>

Free: Obviously, having a free website is a huge draw when it comes to initially starting a blog. It lowers the barrier of entry and removes fear of wasted money.

No tech knowledge required: This type of platform is generally designed to be easy-to-use and follow so you do not need to be a tech-guru to use it.

Limited site maintenance required: With wordpress.com you do not need to worry about site maintenance such as update, backup, or website optimization.

<u>Cons</u>

Limited themes available: The fact that is free means your website is unlikely to be unique in appearance. These themes typically have limited features and functionality so they can be restrictive in that sense. Further, free WordPress theme developers are not obliged to reply to support queries and thus there are limited support options available if your website/ theme is not functioning as it should.

No plugins available/limited SEO: If you pay for your website, you can often add in pre-made plugins. These plugins make life a lot easier. For example, you can install plugins that ensure you are using the best Search Engine Optimization (SEO) practices so that your work can be seen by more people and rank higher on search engines.

Pay for upgrades: Following on from the aforementioned point, if you do wish to customize your theme, it will often cost you extra. You may be able to hire somebody to help you with the coding through websites such as Upwork or Fiverr, but these will still cost money. Further, you have to pay extra if you want a personal, premium or business plan. These all include extra benefits.

Limited monetization options: A free version of Wordpress.com does not allow you to sell adverts on your websites.

Limited analytics: Websites often comes with built-in statistics, but you cannot install third-party programs such as Google Analytics which provides far greater detail.

Domain name: Unless you pay extra, you have to keep wordpress.com in your URL (e.g. example.wordpress.com). This can make your website harder to find, and more difficult for people to remember.

Option 2 - Your own personal website (wordpress.org)

Pros

Full control: You are not required to have branding of your host on your website. You can also sell as many ads as you would like and get to keep one-hundred-percent of what you earn from this. Further, unlike Wordpress.com, you can create an ecommerce store to sell physical or digital goods. Finally, you can create a membership site if you wish in which you can restrict access if you want users to pay to see content.

Unlimited customization: You can install a broader range of themes or write your own. You can also access the range of aforementioned plugins that were inaccessible with wordpress.com.

Better SEO: You have the ability to install plugins/ apps that will enable you to maximize your website's SEO and allow you to rank higher in Google search results.

Compatibility: Having your own personal website allows you to link your blogging account to your business with greater ease/ simplicity as you are in complete control.

Support: Though the technical side may seem daunting, there is a large support community online. Today you can access forums, tutorials, and YouTube videos (just to name a few). All have friendly people willing to help you achieve your goals and give advice. If you search for Facebook groups too, you may be surprised at how many people are trying to launch a blog similar to yours and can provide their expertise/ experiences.

Cons
Higher degree of tech knowledge: Unless you have the skills required yourself, starting your own website can mean you need to either hire someone to achieve your goals, or spend a lot of time learning the necessary skills. You will need to find a good web designer, as well as a skilled developer. For a static website, you may be fine just using HTML and CSS. However, for a more dynamic website you will need to know at least one server-side language such as python, ruby or PHP. Alternatively, if you are using your website to store data, you will need to know SQL. Thus, there are lots of things to consider!

Maintenance time: As the owner of the website, it is your job to keep regular backups, prevent SPAM, and ensure your site is updated and optimized at all times. This can be both difficult technically, and time-strenuous.

Cost: These types of blogs incur regular expenses. For websites that attract high levels of traffic, the cost of hosting can consequently be rather expensive. Further, if you want your own domain name, you will have to pay often for that too. The costs really add up, so I recommend you explore the possibilities beforehand!

22

Hosting your blog

The very first step in setting up your very own personal blog will be to search for a suitable hosting provider. A hosting provider, is very simply a company that provides web space where your website will live. You'll have your very own access to that web space in the form of a login, where you will have access to a dashboard which gives you full control over your website and web space. From here you can configure your website, upload files, set up emails related to your blog, as well as many more options.

Even though it is good to think big and to look towards the future, as you're going to be starting out a simple WordPress installation on a basic hosting package will be sufficient. It's still important to carry out a bit of research and compare providers as they all vary in price and all offer different packages.

There are many hosting providers out there to choose from, you've probably heard of some of the big companies around such as Bluehost, 1&1 and GoDaddy. You should think about the following requirements.

Server Reliability
Everyone has heard the saying "Time is Money" therefore server reliability should be an extremely important factor! If, for example, you end up driving huge amounts of traffic to your blog with your quality content and you have monetized it, but your site is not accessible, it will end up costing you in potential revenue.

Auto Installer
It is pretty much standard that hosting providers supply auto installers of all the popular web platforms, including WordPress. So, if you are a non-techie, setting up a WordPress is a breeze. It should be a case of finding the WordPress auto installer from within the dashboard, filling in your blog

details and waiting for the install to finish. Once complete you can then log straight into your website.

Costs

Look carefully at the initial cost and check how much you will be paying for renewal fees. You do not want to fall in love with your website and then realize you cannot afford to renew it for the next year or that you have to rebrand as a result.

As there are so many hosting providers competing against each other, prices will be competitive therefore providers will advertise many deals to grab your attention. Some providers might try to entice you initially with a cheap introductory sign up offer, but watch out, as once the introductory period has finished the price is likely to rise considerably.

Where will your hosting provider be located?

You might find a brilliant hosting package abroad but remember to consider factors such as time zones - if you need to speak to technical support will this be an issue? These days, however, many companies have live 24hr support where you can speak to a technical advisor using a chat box from the providers website, so it should not be as much of an issue.

♀ Tip:

Some providers try to offer added bolt on extras to your hosting package when you initially sign up. Read carefully what they are trying to sell you as these are usually unnecessary.

Customer satisfaction.
If you are still stuck on choosing, it is always worth carrying out a quick search to read reviews on the various providers to help, make your mind up.

When you've finally selected a hosting, company ensure you buy both the hosting package and domain name with the same company. Some providers will even give you 1 free domain if you take out a hosting package with them. This saves confusion later on when renewal fees are due.

If you decide on a hosting provider and you are not completely satisfied there is always the option of transferring both your blog and domain name to another provider. But this can be a lengthy and complex process so it's best to carry out thorough research beforehand.

Are you ready to move on?

□ **I have decided to host my own personal blog**
□ **I have a topic that I'm going to blog about**
□ **I have a name for my blog**
□ **I have a suitable hosting provider**
□ **I have a domain name**

If you can tick all the boxes proceed to the next chapter 'Setting up your blog'.

SETTING UP YOUR BLOG

After completing the planning phase, you should now have a clear picture of your blogging topic and the direction you would like to pursue as well as what you would like to achieve.

This section will guide you through the process on how to move from the planning phase to actually bringing your blog to life. This is likely to be the where you will have to invest most of your time, especially when it comes creating the content for your blog.

Each stage will be laid out in order, so it is important to follow each step carefully. If you are not very tech savvy, then there is plenty of help available when it comes to the initial WordPress installation. Hosting providers are likely to have documentation and help pages, and as mentioned previously, some will live chats. Finally, YouTube is also a great source if you get stuck.

Otherwise, this book will provide a great resource to explore content generation and the WordPress.org framework. Are you feeling confident?

Setting up a separate email address

Before you start your WordPress installation and get carried away with selecting themes and adding features, you should first set up a separate email account related to your blog. You can do this from within the dashboard - simply look for an area that references to setting up new email addresses. Your email address will, in many instances, be the first point of contact to reach you. If you also plan on having multiple social media channels, then your email will be the link between your brand and your blog. As with any business or brand, if you want to be taken seriously it is essential that you make the right first impression; a branded email displays professionalism and adds weight.

Which looks better?

danny_47a@gmail.com or danny@iloveblogging.com

 Tip:

The beginning of the email, everything before the "@" should be carefully considered. Be creative but don't use informal or inappropriate words like blowmegud@ iloveblogging.com. Perhaps try your first name or something related to the topic of your blog.

Installing WordPress

Installing WordPress using an auto-installer is a breeze. Doing so takes away any of the technical knowledge in having to deal with databases and configuration files. Many hosting companies now offer this service. Simply log into your personal control panel provided by your hosting provider and look for words to the effect of auto-installer, one-click install or app centre.

It should essentially be a case of:
- Installing the application
- Enter your website name
- Fill out your username, email address (the one that you just created) and password
- Wait for the installation to finish
- Log in to your account

Once the installation has finished do not forget to map your domain name to your website. Look for "domains" from within the dashboard. Remember, if you get stuck at any point make sure you seek guidance from your hosting provider's support staff.

Now with your website set up, and a professional looking email address, you can now log into your WordPress site by adding "/**wp-admin**" to the end of your domain name like so **www.your-domain-name.com/ wp-admin.** You will then be taken to the login screen where you will be prompted to enter your username/email address and password. From here, you will finally be taken through to the backend of your blog known as the dashboard.

Choosing your theme

WordPress comes supplied with a selection of base themes titled with the name of the year for e.g. Twenty Sixteen, Twenty Seventeen, etc. These are pretty good themes, are well supported, and have been thoroughly tested before being released. However, there are 1000+ of themes available so it totally depends on what you are looking for and the style that you wish to convey. You can opt to pay for a premium theme, but free ones are excellent to get you started. You can browse themes by selecting Appearance Then Themes from the dashboard and browsing through the various featured and popular themes available. Alternatively, you can search the Theme Directory by visiting (**www.wordpress.org/themes/**).

How To:
To install a theme, it is as simple as a click of a button. Once you have decided on a theme that you like the look of, use the Add Themes dash board panel, hover over the theme, and click the install button. Once it has installed, finally hit activate and your theme will be live.

Tip:

If you decide to change themes after you have created and have added all of your content and media, check over all of your pages so that everything displays correctly.

Install a maintenance mode plugin (Optional)

Please note, this is not essential but if you do not want people viewing your website just at as you are in the process of setting it out how you want it to look then you can download a maintenance mode plugin. This creates a temporary holding page that you can customize to prevent people from scouring your site whilst you are preparing your content. Granted, it is unlikely that you will get any visitors straight away though unless you give out your domain name for people to take a look. This is because it takes a few weeks for Google to start indexing pages, and you are not going to be ranking very highly to begin with. More information about installing plugins will be coming up shortly.

Check over settings

As soon as you log in the first thing to do is to head straight to the "Settings" panel located on the left-hand side of the dashboard. Here you will find all of the essential information about your website such as your site title, the URL, your email address, time zones, and many more options for you to edit. It is important to check through each option and make changes where applicable. One important option that you need to change is the permalink settings. Under common settings, select 'Post Name', this will change the structure of how pages will be displayed within the URL. It is very important for SEO and enables your site to be indexed by search engines with ease.

By default, pages are displayed using a unique id that is generated when a new page is created. For example, if you were to create a contact page it might look something like **www.your-domain-name.com/?p=12**, when viewed from the front end. Selecting 'Post Name' under Permalink Settings will convert the **?p=12** into the page title so it will display as **www.your-domain-name.com/contact.** This makes it more easily readable to visitors and for search engines.

Also, hide your development website for the time being. As you're setting everything up you don't want search engines indexing your website whilst it's half built. Go to **Settings** > **Reading** and check the box next to "**Discourage search engines from indexing your site**"; remember to uncheck this before launching your blog.

Decide on a logo

Once you have decided on a name, look into creating a logo. Ensure that the color, font and style will reflect well alongside the theme of your website. You could pay a fee to have one professionally designed on online platforms such as 99 Designs or hire a freelancer from Upwork. However, if you want to keep expenses down you can easily create a simple logo using design software such as Photoshop. Alternatively, you can use a free website such as Canva.com.

Tip:

If you don't have access to Photoshop, download the free trial version. Otherwise you can use open source software such as GIMP.

It is also possible to create a simple text-based logo from within WordPress. You can type the name of your blog in the Settings panel from within the dashboard and then find an attractive font from a free source such as Google Fonts (**https://fonts.google.com**).

If you decide on creating a logo with design software, consider also creating images for your social media profiles. You can find a quick guide for image dimensions on the next page.

Social media image cheat sheet

Profile Image: 180 x 180px
Cover Photo: 820 x 310px

Profile Image: 250 x 250px
Cover image: 1080px x 1080px

Profile Image: 110 x 110px
Photo Size: 1080 x 1080pxm

Profile Image: 400 x 400px
Profile Background: 1584 x 395px

Profile Image: 165 x 165px

Profile Image: 400 x 400px
Header Photo: 1500 x 500px
Stream photo: 440 x 220px

Profile Image: 800 x 800px
Cover Image: 2560 x 1440px

Create the main pages of your blog

Decide on the pages that will make up your blog. These are the static files of your site and provide the framework for your broader website. For example, you need a home page to act as an initial landing page. You may also want an about page where you can tell visitors about yourself, or a product page if you have items to sell, contact page for people to get in touch, privacy policy etc. These are not likely to change very often but can still be updated. Remember to turn off the comments on pages that are not suitable for visitors to comment, such as a contact page. The following are also important and should be considered.

The 404 page

Set up a 404 error page; these come standard with all themes. With time, the amount of pages and posts you have on your site are likely to grow considerably if you are posting frequently. You may even decide to delete old posts or relocate them. A 404 page is important because if a visitor comes across a link to a non-existent post they will be directed to the 404 page informing the visitor that the page they are looking for no longer exists. You might want to style this page yourself and include some helpful links so users can quickly navigate back to the home page or other potentially useful pages.

The legal pages

Privacy Policy
As a minimum, you should provide a privacy policy on your blog. Privacy is a basic human right in most countries, and, there are many laws that protect individuals from information being collected. A privacy policy acts

35

as a document notifying visitors of what information you are collecting about them. Normally, this will be limited to information from third parties such as Google Analytics or Amazon Affiliates. It also shows transparency and creates a level of trust showing exactly what data you are collecting. You can normally find these pages in the websites footer so they are accessible if people wish to view them.

> ## ♀ Tip:
>
> **You can find many legal templates online that you can download for free. Just amend them adding any other details you may wish to include.**

What you should include:
- Business name and location
- What information you're collecting (names, emails, IP addresses)
- How you are safe guarding their information
- The third-party services that are collecting information

Terms and Conditions

If you're looking at selling physical products or services, you will probably want to include a terms and conditions page. This sets out the guidelines, in terms of understanding responsibilities, rights and responsibilities for each party i.e. your business and the customer.

What you should include:
- What products or services you will be providing
- Any guarantees
- Timelines for delivery
- Payment policies

Adding additional functionality through plugins

One of the joys of WordPress is the ability to customize your site. Just like there are thousands of available themes there is also an abundance of plugins that allow you to add pretty much any functionality you like! Within reason of course. There are: e-commerce plugins that convert your site to an online shop. Contact forms that allow visitors to be able to e-mail you. Security plugins to offer assurances that your blog is safe from hackers. Social media buttons to allow visitors to share your content and there are even booking plugins. The list is absolutely endless and provides a multitude of ways to customize your blog. This is one of the reasons WordPress has grown to be so popular. However, you should also bear in mind that it can also be a weakness to the platform as there is an increase in possible security risks.

It might be tempting to add lots of additional functionality through the use of plugins. But do not go plugin crazy! Only use the essential ones that are properly supported and remember to check the reviews. Using too many plugins is also likely to affect the page load speed as it will have to load a lot of additional scripts and make extra database queries.

> ## ♀ Tip:
>
> **Check the theme customization options. A lot of themes come with the ability to customize various settings, so you may not need a certain plugin.**

Like themes, it is possible to search through the plugin directory from within the dashboard. Under the left menu item Plugins, click Add New then simply search for the name of a functionality you want to ass. For example, if you want to add a contact form, search for the term "contact form" and you will be presented with all the available plugins accordingly. When you have decided on the one you like the look of, click Install Now then Activate. Or head to (**www.wordpress.org/plugins/**) to take look through the directory.

It is important to think about what functionality you would like to add to your blog.

A mailing list?
A booking form?
Are you going to sell products?

Plugins that you should be using

Below you will find a brief overview of a few essential plugins that you ought to think about using. They are all very popular, well supported, and will benefit your blog.

Akismet   **Free,** with also a premium option available.

Akismet comes already installed with WordPress and should be used regularly. Once your blog grows, you will unfortunately and unavoidably become inundated with spam. To prevent this, all of your comments and contact form submissions will be checked against a global database to ensure your website will not display any malicious content. All comments will be filtered and you can view them in the 'comments' panel within the dashboard, this will allow you to sort through and approve legitimate comments. This is a free plugin for blogs and personal sites. However, there is a premium for businesses.

More information can be found at (**www.wordpress.org/plugins/akismet/**).

Yoast SEO   Free, with also a premium option available.

Yoast SEO is a favorite of millions of users and is one of the most popular plugins available. It provides you with the necessary information to improve your ranking in search engines. At the bottom of each page, and the bottom of each post, you will find a traffic light system with handy hints and guidance on how you can improve your content for users and how to make your pages rank better.

More information can be found at (**www.wordpress.org/plugins/wordpress-seo/**).

W3 Total Cache   Free.

W3 Total Cache is another plugin that has been used by millions of users. Running your blog over the coming months and years, your site will likely grow considerably, so site performance is something that should be taken seriously as it is a key factor in getting ranked by Google. W3 Total Cache offers functionality such as minimizing your website files and caching pages allowing for quicker delivery to your readers.

More information can be found at (**www.wordpress.org/plugins/w3-total-cache**).

Contact Form 7   **Free.**

If you are going to be selling products or services, it is highly likely you are going to need a contact form for readers to get in touch. Contact Form 7 is the go-to plugin for this. You are able to create multiple contact forms and can customize and add any form fields that you like. It also supports CAPTCHA and works with Akismet spam filtering. Once you create a form, simply add the short code, something like [**contact-form-7 id="50" title="Contact form 1"**] to the page that you wish to display the form on.

More information can be found at
(**www.wordpress.org/plugins/contact-form-7**).

Social Warfare   **Free**, with a premium option also available.

You want readers sharing your great content and spreading the word. Social Warfare adds social media icons to each page, you can choose where they are positioned and include all the top social media sharing platforms. When a visitor likes a particular post, they can click the social button and your content will be shared.

More information can be found at
(**www.wordpress.org/plugins/social-warfare**)

Updraft   **Free,** with also a premium option available.

Above any other plugin this is probably the most important! Updraft Plus tacks backups of your website. In the unfortunate event that you accidently, for example, delete an essential theme file and break your website, with the click of a button Updraft allows you to easily revert back to a previous site when everything worked correctly. Thankfully, you are able to save backups to many different cloud services such as Dropbox, Google Drive, and Amazon.

More information can be found at
(www.wordpress.org/plugins/updraftplus).

Google Analytics Dashboard for WP (GADWP)   Free.

Google Analytics is a great tool for finding out how many visitors are actually coming to your site, as well as lots of other important information, such as how they got to your blog. GADWP links up with your google analytics page and provides key information from within your WordPress installation dashboard. This cuts out the need of having to log into Google Analytics. Everything can be seen from within your blog.

More information can be found at
(www.wordpress.org/plugins/google-analytics-dashboard-for-wp).

Mail Poet   Free, with a premium option also available.

Email marketing generates a massive amount traffic so you should get a newsletter subscription form set up straight away. Mail Poet is a great plugin for this. It provides a form and the ability to create custom newsletters that you can style how you like using a drag and drop editor. Once you have your newsletter ready to go, all you need to do is select the email list you wish to send your newsletter to.

More information can be found at
(https://wordpress.org/plugins/mailpoet).

Great. Now you have installed some of these, what is next?

Carry out keyword research

Keyword research is the sacred tool to optimizing your blog for search engines. The knowledge used can help to inform both marketing and content strategy. Ultimately, ranking for the right keywords can propel your blog into another dimension. By researching what keywords are in demand, you can determine what you should be focusing on and learn more about your customers generally. At the end of the day, you should not only aim to attract any old visitor but visitors that are interested in your topic and thus visitors that are likely to return – else you will have an astoundingly high bounce rate.

Start by making a list of what topics you believe best represent what is on your blog; put yourself in the shoes of the 'buyer'. What would people search for in order to find the content on your website? Once you have done this, fill each of these topics with keywords to represent what would be within it. For example, if you have 'Bikes' as a keyword, more specific phrases may include 'How to repair a puncture' for example. Just brainstorm for now and narrow the list down later on.

Another way to come up with ideas, especially if you have been blogging for a while now, is to visit Google Analytics and see how your website is already being found. If these are the type of users you believe you would like to focus on, you may enhance existing posts to reflect these demands. For the next step, take the lists you have created and use Google AdWords Keyword Planner Tool to determine what keywords are in demand (**http://adwords.google.com/keywordplanner/**). This process can help you build new campaigns or expand existing ones. Google allows you to get historical statistics on how the keywords have performed, and shows you how they might do in the future, and can also create a new keyword list by itself. From here, it offers a paid option to feature your website at the top of a keyword search so you can track impressions and the conversation rate over the course of a series of clicks. This will then help you to decide if you want to invest in those keywords further.

Another option to use in conjunction with AdWords is the website Google Trends (**https://trends.google.com/trends/**). Based on Google Search, Google Trends shows how often a particular search-term is used compared to the total search volume across the world – it allows you to break it down by region and language.

Overall, try to avoid really broad phrases such as 'China' alone. Even if you were able to rank for that term, chances are people searching for that will be seeking hugely varied answers to their questions on China. They may be looking for information about politics or population growth but if your blog is on travel they may instantly click off your website. This will lower the amount of long-term users on your website.

Instead, it is best to have a mix of both 'head terms' and 'long-tail' keywords. Head terms are shorter phrases, usually between one and three words – an example may be 'Budget Travel China' – again, they will be harder to rank for as the category will be more competitive, but it is better than having a completely broad phrase. These head terms will help inform your long-term goals.

For the short-term, however, ensure you include long-tail keywords. Aim for longer strings of keywords such as 'Things adventurers can do in Kyoto in December'. Keep it specific. Remember, key words are very important to get your blog and posts noticed and research is key to having and maintaining a popular blog.

Start creating awesome posts

Now comes the hard work! Writing engaging content is what blogging is all about, and what you should spend time mastering. If you are not used to writing, or if it does not come naturally to you, it may take time to get into the swing of things but I guarantee that with practice and feedback, you will soon improve.

> ## ♀ Tip:
>
> **Delete all sample content. You will notice that after installing WordPress, sample content will be generated such as a post entitled 'Hello world' as well as a sample page. Make sure you delete these to avoid these pages eventually being index by search engines.**

Posts are content entries. This is what you will be using periodically to release new articles and encourage conversation. As a bare minimum you should create a minimum of 6 quality posts, ideally within 2 different categories. Ensure that you go into a lot of detail with each post and aim to have at least 2,000 words. A blog post of 500 words just will not cut it if you want to be high ranking in search engines. Spend time thoroughly researching your subject and try to provide sources that you can link to.

This will give both you and your post credibility, which will in turn lead to better leads. It is a good idea to think of questions that people might ask or want to know about your niche topic, then, provide an answer and turn your blog posts into problem solving articles. Don't forget to strategically add those keywords you researched earlier into your content as this will help people find you.

Improving the formatting of your articles

Let it be said that there is a right, and a wrong way, to format your posts. When it comes to content marketing, appearances are everything. Taking a bit of extra care in how you format your blog posts will overall dramatically improve your visitor engagement. This can mean the difference between website visitors who convert into leads and readers who leave.

Once you have carried out the hard work of writing your blog posts, formatting is relatively easy and can be considerably swift compared to writing the post itself. Follow the steps laid out below and in the examples on the next page to improve your articles dramatically. Using dummy text, we will compare the right and wrong way to produce an article as a way to show you some quick and easy tips on how to improve.

The wrong way

You can see in the first example there is no formatting whatsoever; this makes the post very hard to read. It is likely that anybody who come across this article would most probably not complete it, or leave the web page straight away.

The correct way

To start with, break your article into small paragraphs. You will see in the second example that this makes a huge amount of difference in the readability. Next, look at the formatting of the text. Read through the post and highlight any key phrases in bold or italic, these can include products, names, or important points that you want to emphasize. This will draw the reader's eyes straight in. It is also a good idea to insert some eye-catching pictures related to the post. This will be covered in more detail below. Finally, add some embedded links on meaningful text as a call to action and have them link to other pages on your blog or away to other websites related to the text.

Other things you can consider are having graphs to represent data, or bulleted lists as these will stand out when readers skim your content.

Example: The incorrect way

HOW TO BECOME A BLOGGER, AN EASY STEP BY STEP GUIDE.

Lorem ipsum dolor sit amet, consectetur adipiscing elit. Aliquam ac est vel nibh elementum dictum. Nunc rhoncus nulla at tortor pretium ultrices. Vivamus consequat mi vel tempus vehicula. Praesent tristique, felis non ornare mollis, tortor enim fringilla quam, quis fringilla nisl lectus eu erat. In sed imperdiet mauris. Aliquam eu libero id odio porttitor varius. Mauris pellentesque urna id lorem cursus, eu sodales neque aliquam. Etiam et faucibus tellus. Morbi sem ante, hendrerit eu dolor at, efficitur dignissim ligula. Vestibulum nibh nibh, tristique nec hendrerit eget, placerat ac enim. In quam neque, scelerisque ut turpis a, facilisis efficitur quam. In hac habitasse platea dictumst. Nunc pretium gravida vestibulum. Suspendisse at diam magna.Ut venenatis dui rutrum purus fermentum mattis. Donec metus ligula, posuere nec mi et, commodo iaculis orci. Cras facilisis eros vel semper vehicula Molorrum sunt ventis repro et et mostrum quiaern atquam enduci test fugit porrum ex evenditae consequam ipidisquaes qui od qui officid untius dus sanis et autemporat optatibus aut res cum accume et evellendae veligeni blandigent. Nis arum dolo eic to exces velecto magnis eos natus moloreptatem iduntin rehenisti alique nonem deliquas dipsaerferia si dolorepudit, adicia velloratent lam non et aspersped eum comnit ipsae vendelitat arum que proritae licipsant, voluptaquam cusdae

Example: The Correct Way

How to become a blogger, an EASY step by step guide.

Lorem ipsum dolor sit amet, consectetur adipiscing elit. Aliquam ac est vel nibh elementum dictum. Nunc rhoncus nulla at tortor pretium ultrices. Vivamus **consequat** mi vel tempus vehicula. Praesent tristique, felis non ornare mollis, tortor enim fringilla quam, quis fringilla nisl lectus eu erat. In sed imperdiet mauris. Aliquam eu *libero id odio porttitor* varius.

Etiam et faucibus tellus.

1. Mauris pellentesque urna id lorem cursus, eu sodales neque aliquam. **Etiam et faucibus tellus.** Morbi sem ante, hendrerit eu dolor at, efficitur dignissim ligula.

2. Vestibulum nibh nibh, tristique nec hendrerit eget, placerat ac enim. In quam neque, scelerisque **ut turpis** a, facilisis efficitur quam. In hac habitasse platea dictumst. Nunc pretium gravida vestibulum.

3. Suspendisse at diam magna.Ut venenatis dui rutrum purus fermentum mattis. Donec metus ligula, posuere nec mi et, commodo iaculis orci. Cras facilisis *eros vel semper* vehicula. Donec **euismod** dui vel justo ornare volutpat.

Adding media to your posts

The media library is where all of your images, videos, recordings, and documents will be stored. Uploading them is easy. You can either navigate to Media within the dashboard and then manually select a file to upload it, or drag and drop images from their location to the library. Alternatively, you can add them as you go. When you are creating a post, look for the "Add Media" button above the text box on the post creation page.

Once you upload your media, whether it be images or documents, you will be able to easily add it to blog posts. However, before you upload any images, check the file size first – more information on this can be found in the upcoming 'Prepare to Launch' section.

Craft killer headlines

Just as it is important to write quality content, a creative headline is equally essential! The headline is the first thing that a visitor will see, and will likely determine whether the reader will carry on reading your post. There is no point in spending the time writing a 2000+ word article if the headline is not going to intrigue readers and leave them wanting to find out more. Resultantly, you want something that jumps out and grabs their attention. You should start by looking at magazines and other blog headlines to get some inspiration.

Have a go at the following exercise on the next page to come up a few headlines of your own.

✏ Exercise

Using the structure below write out 5 different headlines. Try and add in numbers, adjectives and trigger words using different combinations and then read them back.

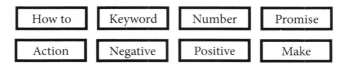

How to	Keyword	Number	Promise
Action	Negative	Positive	Make

E.g.

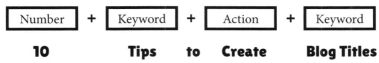

Number	+	Keyword	+	Action	+	Keyword
10		**Tips**	**to**	**Create**		**Blog Titles**

1.

2.

3.

4.

5.

Give every page and post unique meta data

To understand what meta data is, and why it is important to get right, let us first explore the basics. Certain information about a web page (HTML document) can be assigned as meta data. This provides information to search engines on what the page is about and gives instructions to the web browser. There are numerous meta tags available, including:

```
<meta charset="UTF-8">
<meta name="description" content="How to start a blog">
<meta name="keywords" content="blogger, blogging for beginners">
<meta name="author" content="Start Flourishing">
```

Although search engines state that meta data does not provide any ranking benefit, they are still essential and should not be ignored. Meta tags serve the important task in getting visitors from search engines to click through to your website, it is the information within the meta tags, notably the title and description, that is displayed in the search engine results. Click through rate is very important as the more people that click through to your blog, the higher up in search engine rankings you will appear.

Title
```
<title>Start Flourishing | www.start-flourishing.com</title>
```

The title tag is not strictly a meta tag. However, this is going to be the first piece of information that search engine spiders will see when finding out more about your site. It is also the first piece of information that potential visitors will see in search engine results.

Description tag
```
<meta name="description" content="How to start a blog">
```

The description meta tag plays the part of providing a brief snippet on the nature of the page. Its main role, like the title tag, is to educate visitors on what to expect as it displays below the title in search engine results. Now, you can hopefully understand why crafting clever and unique titles and headlines is so important. As a general rule of thumb aim for a 70 character limit for titles and 160 characters for descriptions, ensuring you insert your focus keyword in both.

Below is an example of a search result for the contact page for **www.start-flourishing.com**

Example:

Contact Me | Start Flourishing
www.start-flourishing.com/contact-me
Get in touch, if you'd like to. Any questions that you have I'd gladly answer as swiftly as I can. I'd always welcome your feedback on what you liked about the site, if there was anything you'd like to see more of or if you'd like to see any Improvements to any of the resources.

So, how do you assign unique meta data?
Relax, you do not have to worry about learning to code. This is where the aforementioned Yoast SEO plugin comes in. Yoast SEO allows you to assign custom meta descriptions and titles to every single page, post, archive, and taxonomy within your website.   When you activate the plugin and go to a page or post and scroll down, you should notice a box where you'll be able to enter a keyword, determined by the aforementioned keyword research you should have conducted. Here you shold come up with a creative title and description. When you save the page, Yoast SEO will automatically add the meta information to the code behind the scenes.   You are even

provided with a traffic light system as a visual guide to ensure you are fully optimizing each page to rank better; green being good, red being poor.

Create your social profiles.

Social media is a massive driving force in getting traffic to your blog. You want your posts to get seen and shared by as many people as possible and there are very big communities and niche groups to be found across all platforms. It is important to consequently set up the channels you intend to use.

Do not get bogged down in setting up accounts for every single platform out there. It will be extremely time consuming and could become quite confusing trying to manage so many accounts. Instead, select a few and concentrate on building up a following with them. Some platforms are better than others. For example, Facebook pages tend not to fare well for bloggers unless you have a closed group where you are constantly engaging with people to keep the group active. Whereas a Facebook business page might do better for products that you're selling as you can target specific groups in your niche.

There are also scheduling platforms available, Hootsuite is one example where you can link a number of your social media accounts too one manageable place as it allows you to create and schedule posts for a future date. This is great in freeing up your time as you can put aside a few hours one day a week to prepare your posts and then schedule them to be drip fed throughout the week.

Set Up Summary

If you have made it this far congratulations! You now have a fully working blog. Now that you are set up, spend some time playing around with the dashboard. Learn how to create, edit, and delete pages as well as how to add and remove images. It is often simply a matter of playing around and learning where everything is, but try not to break anything! Learning how to take backups will be covered in the next section. Taking backups will allow you to recover a previous state should the worse happen to your blog.

Are you ready to prepare to launch?

☐ **I have a professional looking email address related to my blog**
☐ **I have a WordPress Installation set up**
☐ **I have customized my blog to my liking**
☐ **I have created a great logo**
☐ **I have set up all of the landing pages**
☐ **I have a 404 page, contact page and legal pages**
☐ **I have created at least 6 posts within 2 categories**
☐ **I have provided unique meta data for every post and page**
☐ **I have created my social media profiles**

If you tick all the boxes proceed to the chapter entitled: 'Prepare to launch'.

PREPARE TO LAUNCH

For some of you, the setup phase would have been a steep learning curve, and others a breeze but hopefully you managed to come through with minimal issues? Congratulations you should now have a fully working personal blog and be ready to move onto the next stage.

From here you will be applying the finishing touches so that you can launch your blog and start attracting visitors. In this section, we will delve into exploring analytics, how to optimize your blog to track your visitor's habits and how to carry out testing so that your blog is compatible on all the major browsers.

By the end of this chapter you will be able to hit the live button, metaphorically speaking, and propel your personal blog out to millions of potential readers.

Let's start applying the finishing touches.

Sign up to Google Analytics and Google Search Tools

GOOGLE ANALYTICS

Both Google Analytics and Google Search Tools are great utilities for gathering information. Of course, you are going to want your blog to be seen by as many people as possible. When you are putting in all that hard work to drive traffic to your blog, how do you know what is working and what is not? Here is where Google Analytics comes in. Do you want to know the best thing about it? It is completely **FREE!**

So, what actually are analytics?

Analytics is quite simply the data that is collected about the activities of visitors to your website; it tracks and reports on website traffic. This can become extremely useful when tailoring various marketing campaigns.

What can Google Analytics tell you?

Google Analytics provides an abundance of data in the form of reports. It might seem very overwhelming to begin with but it is best to break it down further and to try and understand a little bit more about each of the different types of reports available. These reports are categorised into a number of sections that you can find on the left-hand side within the Google Analytic Dashboard under Reports. Below, you will find a brief overview of each section explaining both the purpose, and the type of data collected.

Real Time: Real Time allows you to view your blog activity as it happens. You will be able to see the reports being updated literally seconds after an event occurs – this can show you how many people are on your blog right now, what pages they are on, and whether/ what conversions have occurred.

Audience: Audience provides information on the actual visitors that are coming to your blog. You can find out information such as their location, operating system, what browser they use, and what kind of device they were on (whether it be mobile, tablet, or desktop).

Acquisition: Acquisition refers to how your visitors are actually getting to your blog and what they do once they are there. It also provides an insight on conversion data such as how many of your visitors are buying products or filling out a form for example. This is a great for looking at which channels are working for driving traffic to your blog. By clicking on referrals, you can see, for instance, how many users came from your social media channels.

Behavior: Behavior provides an insight into how the individual pages of your blog perform. Providing information on page views, the average time spent on each page, the exit rate, and the bounce figure.

Conversions: Conversions are the desired actions you want your readers to take. For example, getting someone to fill out a contact form, or following through with making a purchase.

How do I install Google Analytics?

Now you are a little more familiar on the type of information that you can harness within Google Analytics lets install your tracking code to your blog.

You can add Google Analytics to your website using one of the many plugins available. However, as mentioned earlier, you should limit the number of plugins you use and so it is advisable to add tracking code into your theme files without a plugin as it can be done with relative ease.

Once you have signed up to Google Analytics and logged in, click on "Admin". From the drop down under "Account" click on "Create a New Account" and fill out all the required information. Finally click on the blue button "Get Tracking ID" to get your tracking code. Highlight the code and right-click to copy it. We will add it to your blog in the next step.

Head back to your blog's dashboard and from here go to "Appearance" then "editor" from the left-hand menu ensure you select the header.php file from the right hand menu. Next, simply paste the tracking code right before the closing **</head>** tag and finally click the Update File button.

Example of a tracking code:

```
<!-- Google Analytics -->
<script>
(function(i,s,o,g,r,a,m){i['GoogleAnalyticsObject']=r;i[r]=i[r]||function(){
(i[r].q=i[r].q||[]).push(arguments)},i[r].l=1*new Date();a=s.createElement(o),
m=s.getElementsByTagName(o)[0];a.async=1;a.src=g;m.parentNode.
insertBefore(a,m)
})(window,document,'script','https://www.google-analytics.com/analytics.js','ga');
ga('create', 'UA-XXXXX-Y', 'auto');
ga('send', 'pageview');
</script>
<!-- End Google Analytics -->
```

GOOGLE SEARCH TOOLS

Google also provides Google Search Console free of charge. This tool allows you to see information about how well your website is being indexed in Google's search results. In turn, this can provide insight on how you can optimize your blog's visibility.

How can I add my blog to Google Search Console?

To begin with you need to show that you are the actual owner of your blog thus you must verify it with Google. To do this, log in to the Search Console and click on "Add Property" button, provide your blog's URL, and click "add".

Next, you need to add a HTML meta tag to your blog's home page. This can be done by the exact same process as how you added your Google

Analytics tracking code. Go to the header.php file and paste it underneath the last of the other meta tags. Remember to click "Update File". Go back to the Search console where you copied the meta tag and click "Verify" to finally verify your site.

Note, it does take time for the Search Console to gather and process the information for your blog so do not expect to see any data straight away.

Add social media buttons

Placing social media buttons on your blog is another very important aspect of blogging as they are valuable tools for promoting your content, which is ultimately what you want your readers to be doing.

By placing buttons, you can also get an indication of what topics are more popular than others. This will give you an insight on subjects that you should concentrate on.

You will most likely come across 2 types of buttons, those that allow you to follower users, and those that allow you to share posts. But how do you know which ones to place where? Understanding both types of buttons and the difference between them will help you in knowing where to best situate the buttons for maximum effect. Let us look at each one in further detail.

SOCIAL MEDIA FOLLOW BUTTONS

Follow buttons allow fans to keep up-to-date with your website at all times. Instead of having to check up on your website constantly, they may be reminded to visit by having you appear on their personal homepage instead. Consequently, it allows you to promote your presence across various social networks with greater ease and to those who already wish to visit your website. Remember to only have follow links to the accounts that you will actually plan on using as this will keep your blog looking clean and avoid misleading the user or having broken links on your webpage. You could place these buttons anywhere on your blog but they are better positioned on the landing pages such as your 'About' page or 'Home' page side bar.

SOCIAL MEDIA SHARE BUTTONS

Share buttons spread your content around the wider web. Share buttons allow visitors to easily share your content across their own networks and in turn help attract new audiences to your blog.

These buttons are more suited to being placed on individual posts. After all, the content of your posts will be what attracts visitors, and, in turn increases traffic to your website.

The aforementioned 'Social Warfare' plugin is a great short-term solution for placing social media sharing buttons to your blog. This tool allows you to place social media buttons from some of the top social networks including:

- Facebook
- Twitter
- Google+
- Pinterest
- LinkedIn
- StumbleUpon

You also have the ability to place share buttons where you want them to show up, whether it be above or below the post content. Just make sure its visible and easy to use.

Carry out testing

One of the primary reasons for going over your blog with a fine toothcomb and testing everything works correctly is due to the levels of competition in blogging. No doubt there will be other websites offering similar information to yours. If there happened to be an error on the page, or if a visitor cannot easily find what they are looking for, they will naturally proceed to another site. Consequently, even if your blog looks beautiful, it is pointless if visitors cannot navigate easily around your site as it may put people off returning.

What testing do I need to carry out?

CHECK YOUR WEBSITE ON ALL MAJOR BROWSERS - CHROME, FIREFOX, SAFARI, EDGE, AND OPERA.

The whole purpose of testing your blog across multiple web browsers is to ensure it renders correctly in any browser. There are many web browsers now available, some more popular than others. We all have our favorite browser that we use all the time. So it is important to cater for everyone. Chrome still has the highest market share at 58% followed by Safari, Firefox, Edge, and Opera - each coming with their advantages and disadvantages. Since each browser uses different rendering engines, results can vary. A page displayed in Chrome, for instance, could look different in Firefox as some coding methods might not be supported yet.

To test this you can easily download all the latest browsers and carry out a visual check of all your pages. Another alternative is using an online platform such as (**www.browsershots.org**). You can enter your blog URL and choose the browser versions to test on. When you click submit you will be presented with a snapshot of how it looks in various web browsers that you selected.

CHECK YOU BLOG ON DIFFERENT DEVICES.

Smartphones, tablets, notebooks, laptops and desktop computers are just some of the devices that we use to connect to the internet. Users of smartphones, however, now account for the majority of internet users in numerous nations worldwide. You should therefore pay extra attention to ensure your blog is optimized for smartphones.

Things to consider

Check over the look and flow of the pages and check that spacing between image and text look right. Ensure images and text blocks do not and think about if you need to hide unimportant information for mobile devices. Finally, consider whether all of the text be seen clearly; is it big enough?

ENSURE YOUR 404 PAGE IS WORKING CORRECTLY.

You should also test that your 404 page is working correctly. Go to your blog and in the URL type 404.php after the domain name e.g. **www.start-flourishing.com/404.php**.

TEST YOUR CONTACT FORM

It is likely that you will want people to contact you. There is nothing quite like hearing how you have helped someone out with the advice you have provided. Even more so if you have some kind of service or product to offer. It is thus vital to ensure your contact form is working correctly. Go through the process of filling in every field and submitting a message. Also see what happens when you do not fill in certain fields.

Things to consider

- After submitting the form, is the correct thank you message displayed?
- Is there validation on required form fields?
- Does the email go to the correct address?

WEBSITE PERFORMANCE TEST

As briefly touched upon in the chapter on setting up your blog, the page load time (that is, the speed at which it takes for a web page to display content) should be of the upmost importance; every second counts. Understandably, the average user has little patience for a page that is taking ages to load. Research shows that 40% of users abandon a website that has not loaded within 3 seconds. Google has even indicated that its algorithm uses speed as a key factor to decide where to rank your site.

How can I decrease page load time?

Here are a few simple steps to save precious seconds.

File Compression

Here's where the W3 Total Cache plugin comes into play. You can use this to minify all your blog's files. Using W3 Total Cache optimizes your files, it removes all the spaces, commas, comments, and needless characters from the code, thus reducing file size.

Optimize Images

Images are going to be a big part of driving engagement. Having images makes your blog look visually appealing and helps with search engine traffic. Opt for high quality images but do not exceed 500kb in file size as they will be the biggest files for the browser to load. Before you move your images to your media library, just check the file size and even run it through an online image optimization, such as tinypng (**https://tinypng. com**). This website selectively removes the number of colors in the image without loss of quality.

Tip:

To get an idea of how quickly it takes for your site to load run it through a speed test using (https://tools.pingdom. com).

Remove Unnecessary Files

At first, you might be excited to download and try out the many plugins on offer. However, if you find you are not using some of them, get rid of them! Having too many will only make it harder to manage and have the burden of more resources to load; that goes for themes as well.

Validate your blog

In the early days of the web, developers had their own ways of doing things. The chances of a website being compatible with all browsers was almost inconceivable. As a result, a set of web standards were brought in to provide a basis for order. Consequently, validation is regarded as one of the most important aspects of building a website. A website that has been designed and built to the specifications laid down in the web standards means the code is compliant and will work without any problems. Validation is also going to make you blog fair better in search ranking.

You can run your site's URL through the online W3C validators below as you will get an idea of any major errors that may need rectifying.

HTML Validator: https://validator.w3.org

CSS Validator: https://jigsaw.w3.org/css-validator

As WordPress is built upon its own framework it has its own set of coding standards to abide by. If you are using a readymade theme it should be already coded to web standards but, for an additional test, you can download the plugin Theme Check (**www.wordpress.org/plugins/theme-check/**). This plugin will test the validation of your WordPress theme and checks it is supported with the latest version of WordPress. Once installed you can run an automated test through an admin panel. This is more for theme developers but there is no harm in wanting to double check your own theme.

Favicon

As you browse the web you will notice a little icon in the tab of the web browser window, this is known as a favicon. Favicons are not essential, so what's the point in having one then?

They do serve the role of adding the finishing touches to not only your blog but to your brand too. When a visitor opens your site, a favicon provides an indicator that they are at the right place. There is always the added bonus that if anyone has booked marked one of your pages it will be all that easier and quicker to look for.

Creating a favicon is a straightforward process, you can either create one by using image editing software or going to a free online favicon generator. Create whatever design you wish but remember to keep it very simple as it is very tiny. Resize the image to 16px x 16px and save the image as "**favicon.ico**" to your desktop.

Important! Schedule regular backups

Your WordPress blog is a pretty sophisticated platform with lots of interconnected files that ensure it runs properly. Practically every professional website, blog or e-commerce platform is in some way going to be connected to a database where data can be stored, accessed, and displayed in some manner. After all, it is the data that what attracts visitors to your site. So, what can you do to protect all those files and all that very important data?

You can pretty much buy insurance for anything that will protect you against an unfortunate event: personal injury insurance, home insurance, motor insurance. So, why not get insurance for your website? Taking regular backups basically acts as your insurance and it is free! It covers you against any mishaps that you might personally cause by deleting things you should not be messing with, and even against possible attacks by hackers. You could have your site back up and running with a click of a button should the worst happen.

♀ Tip:

Don't rely on your hosting provider to provide backups. It's down to you to set up.

How do I take regular backups?

1. Start by downloading the aforementioned Updraft plugin. Under **Set Up**, click activate.

2. Head to **Settings** and under UpdraftPlus Backups select its personal **Settings** tab.

67

3. Configure how often you want your backups to run. Once you have your blog set up it is probably unlikely that you will be changing the files often. In this case, you may want to back up files on a weekly basis rather than daily. The database schedule though, is where obviously all the data is stored. If you are making daily updates to your blog then you should ensure you select daily backups.

4. Choose your remote storage facility and enter the connection details then choose what files you want to be included in backups. The remote storage is where all your backup WordPress files and database file will be stored. Dropbox is great for this!

5. Save Changes.

6. Go to the **Current Status** tab and click **Back Up Now**.

You are now fully backed up. Should anything bad happen, all you have to do is click the Restore button to reactivate the last saved state of your installation.

Discourage search engines from indexing your blog

Finally, if you ticked the 'Engine Visibility' checkbox earlier during the set-up phase, you can now untick it as you are ready for your blog to start being indexed. Your blog won't appear in search results straight away; it will take time for search engines to crawl your site. In the meantime, begin thinking about your next blog posts and start working on your campaigns to driving traffic.

Prepare to launch summary

Great! You have come so far – now is not the time to give up but to persevere. Remember, utilize tools such as Google Analytics and Google Search to ensure you make the most of your keyword research. Social media buttons will also really help propel your blog into the wider web and make it more accessible to a wider range of people. Before you launch, testing your website on different devices will enable you to ensure every user has the best possible experience and enjoys easily reading what you have to say. Finally, remember to add the finishes touches such as a favicon and ensure you keep regular backups – accidents are unforeseeable for a reason. Insure yourself and your work against such mistakes. Good luck!

MAINTAINING

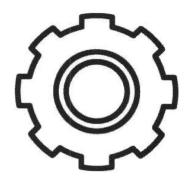

The prepare to launch phase centered around quality control where we went in to greater details about launching your blog to a high standard.

If you followed the steps you should now be in a position where you shouldn't have to make any more major alterations. It is all about maintaining your blog which is in itself fairly simple in theory, yet can become complex as it is all about keeping your blog secure, driving traffic through campaigns, and continue to create great posts.

Blog security

Maintaining the security of your blog is paramount. WordPress is without doubt the most popular content management system out there, and with such popularity comes with it the threat of being targeted by hackers.

So how can you keep your site safe?

WordPress regularly release maintenance and security updates to the core framework. You should always update these once released as potential hackers could have found vulnerabilities in the previous version. Similarly, plugins and themes are also regularly amended and these should be updated when given the chance. You will find notifications of updates within the dashboard; it requires a simple click of a button to update.

♀ Tip:

Remember, before you carry out any updates make sure you have backed up your blog so you can roll back to a previous version in case anything brakes.

Reply to comments

When you start receiving comments, you are likely to feel inspired as it shows that visitors are coming to your site. It might be hard to tell whether they are actually spam or legitimate but you should consider replying to every comment. Commenters want to get that feeling that their opinion is being listened to.

Your replies will also be displayed underneath your posts. Other visitors will see this so it can lead to potential interactions from other visitors. It won't look good, however, and could put people off returning if there are a lot of questions and feedback from people yet no replies from you.

It is up to you how you respond to e-mails or comments. You may decide to update the post to provide answers or to respond individually but remember to handle each comment in a polite manner even if you both have opposite views.

Observe analytics

Using and understanding analytics are key factors in helping to gauge how successful your blog is. You can gather massive amounts of information. Though it might seem overwhelming to begin with, when you start to understand the data you can start to understand the behavior of visitors. In turn, this will allow you to tailor and optimize your website for better results and to help drive future campaigns.

Today, you can also find analytics on many of the social media sites too. If you set up a Pinterest business page, for example, you can gain an insight into those that are saving and clicking on both your boards and pins. Similarly, a business account with Instagram gives statistics on impressions, the age and gender of followers, and the number of profile views you have over a certain period of time.

Do you remember the type of data that can be collected? Let us refresh:

**Who is visiting
How many are visiting
How they got there
What pages are most popular
What devices they're using
How long they stayed**

Be consistent and improve your writing

Being consistent requires careful planning. Aim to set out a schedule of when you will be posting new content and stick to it. When you have built up a devout following and they become deeply excited for your weekly post, how are readers going to feel when it finally arrives a month late?

How often do you plan on publishing weekly, monthly?

Writing does take a lot of effort but the burden can be lifted with the planning that you put in to each of your articles. Staring at a blank document might seem terrifying. To get started, firstly choose a topic that is obviously related to your blog and think about some questions that readers might want answering.

Once you have some questions, you can then begin to create suitable headings as this will break your blog post down into accomplishable sections. Proceed to work diligently on each individual section. Write about whatever comes into your mind - forget about grammar, punctuation, or spelling mistakes and just get the main body of your copy down. This will give you something to work with. Later, you can go back over your post and fix all the errors.

The benefits of consistent blogging include:

- Your SEO ranking will shoot up
- Generate more great ideas
- Your following will continue to grow and your readers will be impressed

You may already be an expert on your subject but do not forget to continually carry out research with whatever subject you are writing about. Even if you are posting your own views on a topic, it is still important to provide helpful references to back up the information you are presenting.

Once you feel that you have completed a blog post, do not publish it! Leave it a day or two then come back with a fresh set of eyes and re-read it. You may instantly notice some vital information that you feel necessary to include. If possible, it would be great to get a friend or family member to take a look over it.

Ideally you should write daily. It does not matter whether you will be publishing posts to your blog weekly, bi-weekly, or monthly. Try to get into the habit of writing most days, not just when you are feeling in the mood or inspired. This way you will continue to increase your writing speed, work on your skills, and improve the quality of your writing.

♀ Tip:

Aim to start writing 300 words a day. When you find that becomes easy, then increase to 600 and so on.

Consider vlogging

Vlogging (Video Blogging) is not going to be for everyone, especially for those uncomfortable in front of a camera. Vlogging is very simply filming yourself, talking about your ideas, opinions, experiences, and information on your niche topic, then uploading those videos to platforms such as YouTube. Video blogs have become extremely popular with some YouTube channels bringing in tens of thousands, and even millions of views.

Vlogs offer a great way to present visual content that is a lot quicker to process. It is much easier to sit and watch a video than to read a long article. Vlogs also allow for a deeper connection on an intimate level, in the sense that it allows viewers a private view into your world.

If you go down the vlogging route it is just as important to plan what you are going to talk about and how you go about it. Look at what others are doing: how do they address their audiences? Consider writing a rough script of points you want to cover. You can be equally creative with vlogs by changing up the locations or filming techniques for example.

Vlogs are likely to be more time-consuming than writing blog posts as it takes a lot of time to film re-takes and edit a final cut. Of course, there additional cost involved too. You will want to invest in video recording equipment and specialist editing software to put out quality content. However, you do not have to pay domain fees or other associated website fees as using YouTube as a platform is free of charge.

Develop new campaigns to drive traffic

Continue to establish innovative ideas that will generate new leads. You want to be looking at constantly evolving your blog to keep it fresh and up-to-date. Keep track of the latest trends and recent news related to your topic and think of ways you could present new blog posts, products or services;

what could you offer that's new?

Discounts to products/services
New downloads
Updated downloads
A new service
Free products/services
Hints and tips

Have in place something to monitor your progress with your new campaigns as this will enable you to see whether it is worth the effort.

When planning new campaigns think about the following:

- What will be your call to action?
- Who are you trying to influence?
- Do you have a budget?
- How are you going to execute your campaigns?

The success of your campaigns will obviously vary depending on what you aim to accomplish. For example, if you want to drive more people to subscribe to your blog you will be able to monitor your mailing lists. If it is to promote a new product, use the tools that come with e-mail marketing as this is great way to get a range of statistics about how many people are reading your emails as well as the click through rate.

Join related forums

It is important to continually reach out and openly attract like-minded people and what better way than to join related forums. Forums are communities that allow people to start discussions on different topics that other members can reply to.

Do not join a forum and simply start posting messages asking people to view your blog, this will just come off as spam and you will likely be instantly banned by the moderators. Forums do normally come with rules. A forum is where people can discuss or get answers to questions; blatant self-promotion is not going to go down well.

Normally you will have a forum signature, an area for a short bio, and profile image where a link to your blog can be added, if it is allowed. It is essentially a small advert which is displayed after every post that you contribute.

In short, look to solve people's questions, be active and add value with your responses to build your credibility. Once you have built up credibility you can then subtly start to promote your blog – if they can find an answer to their question on your blog, for example, you may be able to link to it.

Connect with other bloggers

No doubt you have already carried out some research into the big influencers in your subject. Like joining forums, before reaching out, ensure you have established a relationship. Add value by following and liking posts from blogs that you follow on social media platforms. Leave comments on the blogger's website and continually put in the effort to link to their articles; everybody appreciates their content being shared and would welcome the additional exposure to more traffic. You could even offer your own products or services in exchange for a guest post.

Just be wary that a lot of distinguished bloggers are going to be receiving tons of emails every day from similar people as yourself, responding to every email can be exhausting so make sure you can offer something in return to boost your chances of getting a positive response.

Maintain active social media accounts

We have already touched upon how social media is such a huge driver of traffic. However, it is not going to be enough to just have a profile and to publish the odd post every so often. Maintaining active social media accounts are going to help you in a number of ways.

It will help promote your brand awareness. Social media is a fantastic way of allowing your brand to be seen. Regular posts will allow you to be seen as an authority within your niche and posting often will help keep your brand in the minds of readers.

Get your family and friends on side

It is only natural to want to seek recognition and support for your efforts so reach out to those closest around you. Get them to help out with the small tasks such as sharing posts and leaving positive comments. Also, it might be worthwhile to run your thoughts by them as they could even help to drum up some creative ideas for you next blog posts.

Enjoy it

Finally, learn to enjoy it! Enjoy reaching out to readers, learning new skills, and improving yourself. It is a real achievement to be proud of.

MAKE MONEY

To successfully make money from your blog requires time and patience. Do not initially go into blogging with the sole intention of making money as you will more than likely lose interest after time and eventually fail. Driving a lot of traffic to your site and building your mailing list takes a lot of hard work. Start a blog because you have a deep interest in your chosen subject and you want to help and inform people, see it as a hobby; think about monetization as an added bonus.

Of course, there are many examples out there of people making a very successful living out of blogging. You can find many bloggers who are very transparent in both their revenue and income streams and many release monthly income statements. Take a look at some bloggers you already know, you may even get some ideas on how you can monetize your blog. Below we will look at some of the potential ways open to you.

There are 5 basic steps to create additional income. On the surface, they sound fairly straight forward but once you delve deeper and start trying to implement each step, it can become quite complex and extremely time consuming to implement.

Steps to make money

1. Start by concentrating on attracting visitors
You are going to attract visitors by writing content that people want to read and find interesting, see the chapter on setting up your blog for on how to write great blog posts. Further, remember to try and drive traffic through social media accounts too.

2. Consider giving away freebies such as downloadable PDFs
Give something away for free to draw visitors in. A downloadable worksheet, or a cheat sheet related to your niche for example.

3. Get visitors signed up to a mailing list

When you offer freebies, get people signed up prior to downloading documents. A mailing list allows you to contact your subscribers with offers and products on a recurring basis. Why do you think so many big companies out there get you to sign up before allowing you access to a discount?

4. Continue to send out useful content through a steady stream

As you release frequent content you will start to appear as a leader and knowledgeable in your niche. This, in turn, will build trust. It is important to be completely honest and apologize for any mistakes. It can take years to build a reputation and yet a mere five minutes to lose one.

5. Offer a premium product or service

People buy what they want, not what they need, so create and market something that visitors are going to find useful and appealing.

♀ Tip:

When your blog starts making money it is essentially a small business, so treat it like one. Remember, you are now an entrepreneur.

Do not think that you are limited to just one income stream, there are lots of ways to make extra cash. As a blogger you need to be creative, always thinking up new ways to improve your blog and get creative with making multiple income streams. Diversifying spreads the risk, so you do not have all your eggs in one basket. Let's look at the different types of money streams that you could implement:

WAYS YOU CAN MAKE MONEY WITH YOUR BLOG

Recurring Revenue
- Subscription service
- Premium Content

Services
- Freelancing
- Marketing
- Coaching
- Graphic Design
- Copyrighting
- Training
- Coding

Advertising
- Google AdSense
- Competitions
- Reviewing Products

Other Donations

Products

Virtual
- eBooks
- Online Course
- Apps
- Music
- Games
- Photography

Physical
- Books
- Craft

Events
- Workshops
- Seminars
- Webinars
- Live meet ups

Affiliate Marketing
- Amazon Associates
- Clickbank
- Rakuten

Promoting your side business

Advertising

The easiest place to start would be using ad networks such as Google AdSense. Once you have signed up you have a choice of a multiple banners that can be placed anywhere on your blog. When a visitor clicks on the advert, you get paid a small percentage. However, do not plaster your blog with hundreds of annoying pop up and banner ads it will more than likely be off-putting and drive people away.

When you have developed a substantial following, and have a high amount of traffic coming through your site, you may be approached by companies who are willing to pay for ad space or for you to promote their products.

Note, you are not likely to make much of an income through AdSense, so it is best not to solely rely on this method. However, it is another income stream and it all mounts up.

Affiliate Marketing

Another great starting point for generating income is affiliate marketing. It is essentially linking through to products that are for sale on other websites. If someone clicks through and makes a purchase you earn a small percentage in commission for that sale. You can easily sign up to a lot of the big companies that offer affiliate marketing, Amazon Associates being one of the biggest.

Services

If you have a skill or a creative edge look at providing a service, this could be anything, for example web design, copywriting, or tuition services.

Products

Products include both virtual and physical items. There are so many options available in providing products to sell, examples include eBooks, online tutorial courses, branded clothing, artwork, phone apps, jewelry etc. So, get creative and start making items to sell. You could even find additional platforms to list your products on such as Etsy.

Promoting your side business

If you have a successful or growing side business, start driving traffic through your blog to grow your profile.

Recurring Revenue - Membership Site

Having a source of recurring revenue will be extremely lucrative. Your visitors are likely to pay good money to join a membership site providing that you have something to offer that they want and that they may not be able to get elsewhere. Look at offering premium content or a closed area where members can join a community. Or think about creating a service or tool that requires a recurring subscription. Websites such as NomadList or JacksFlights are good examples of this.

If you are going to offer unique content, this is going to take a lot of hard work as you will constantly have to provide new information each month. There are a couple ways you can do this: either by making your own content or compiling information acquired from other sources, the web, or books.

As you can see from the charts on the next page, potentially, you only need to reach between 100 and 200 customers that are willing to pay $5.99 to make a living. Remember though that members are likely to come and go so you are always going to have to work on your strategy to reach out to new members.

Example of a membership site at $5.99

Month	Members	$ Per Month	$ Per Year
5.99	10	59.90	718.80
5.99	20	119.80	1437.60
5.99	30	179.70	5391.00
5.99	40	239.60	2875.20
5.99	50	299.50	3594.00
5.99	60	359.40	4312.80
5.99	70	419.30	5031.60
5.99	80	479.20	5750.40
5.99	90	539.10	6469.20
5.99	100	599.00	7188.00
5.99	250	1497.50	17970.00
5.99	400	2396.00	28752.00
5.99	550	3294.50	39534.00
5.99	700	4193.00	50316.00
5.99	850	5091.50	61098.00
5.99	1000	5990.00	71880.00

Example of a membership site at $19.99

Month	Members	$ Per Month	$ Per Year
19.99	10	199.90	2398.80
19.99	50	399.80	4797.60
19.99	30	599.70	7196.40
19.99	40	799.60	9595.20
19.99	50	999.50	11994.40
19.99	60	1199.40	14392.80
19.99	70	1399.30	16791.60
19.99	80	1599.20	19190.40
19.99	90	1799.10	21589.20
19.99	100	1999.00	23988.00
19.99	250	4997.50	59970.00
19.99	400	7996.00	95952.00
19.99	550	10994.50	131934.00
19.99	700	13993.00	167916.00
19.99	850	16991.50	203898.00
19.99	1000	19990.00	239880.00

Events

Probably for the more established blogger, but another avenue to think about. Set up an event or a convention where like-minded people can meet up, present, and discuss ideas. Consider getting sponsorship from companies or charging people to attend. This could be either in person at a venue or by hosting your own webinar/ online workshop.

Remember, have a think about what you can offer your visitors.

If you have made it this far and have followed the steps outlined in this book, then congratulations! Undoubtedly you have put a tremendous amount of effort into your blog and hopefully have acquired a whole range of new skills. These skills should not only give you personal satisfaction, but know that today they are in high demand. If you have learnt how to utilize Google Analytics or harness the power of social media, you have successfully joined the millennial job market. There are a whole range of opportunities now open to you.

Alternatively, if you have just finished this book to gain an insight into what is required, then I urge you to jump in and begin this joyful pursuit. Though it can be stressful at times, at the end of it all I promise it will be worth it when it comes to lessons learnt and skills developed upon.

GET INSPIRED, GET CREATIVE, AND GET STUCK IN!

HAPPY BLOGGING!

SETTING UP YOUR BLOG

CHECKLIST

☐ Decide on your blog subject
You have a subject that you are passionate about?

☐ Choose your blogging platform
Do you want full control of your blog?

☐ Compare suitable hosting providers
Compare hosting providers to get the best deal.

☐ Choose a domain name
Decide on a name related to your blog or niche.

☐ Set up an email account related to your blog
An email linked to your blog will look a lot more professional.

☐ Choose a unique password and username for you login
Don't pick admin as a username!

☐ Login to your control panel and use the auto installer to install WordPress
Use the 1 click installation for a fast setup.

☐ Connect your domain name to your WordPress installation
So when visitors type in your domain name they will be directed to your site.

☐ Create a fact sheet with handy URLS (optional)
Keep in a safe place!

☐ Login to your site
Place "/wp-admin" after your domain name to get to the login screen.

☐ **Install a Maintenance mode plugin**
Prevent users from accessing your blog whilst you're preparing it.

☐ **Choose a well-supported theme from the theme directory, (ensure responsive)**
There are 1000s of themes to choose from. Read the reviews and pick a well-supported theme.

☐ **Customise your theme styles to your liking**
Edit you themes colours to match your branding style.

☐ **Check your website credentials**
Check over all the settings from the settings panel within the dashboard.

☐ **Check time zones**
Change the time to your location.

☐ **Delete all the sample content**
You don't want all the sample content to be indexed by search engines.

☐ **Change default category name**
Change "Uncategorized" to something meaningful.

☐ **Set up additional categories**
Create the categories that your blog posts will be grouped in.

☐ **Set permalinks to Post Name**
Do this in production, not on the live site!

☐ **Upload all your media – Images, pdfs etc**
Fill out attachment details.

☐ Check comment settings

Block out spam by having to approve all comments before allowing them on your site.

☐ Configure social media channels

Set up your branded social media channels.

☐ Logo design / font based logo

Design your own brand logo.

☐ Create a 404 page

A helpful response to tell the visitor they've clicked on a broken link.

☐ Add a contact page

Allow visitors to contact you with their questions.

☐ Mailing list

Set up mailing a list to generate leads.

☐ Create at least 6 pages within 2 categories

Aim to make your pages at least 2000 words long.

☐ High quality images for your blog post

Help engagement with quality images about your topic.

☐ Legal pages and ensure links are visible in footer

Privacy policy and T&Cs if you're selling products.

☐ Add useful plugins such as Yoast SEO, Google Analytics

These provide information on how your site is performing and can help your site rank better.

PREPARE TO LAUNCH

CHECKLIST

☐ Social Share Buttons
All your social media buttons are linking to the correct accounts.

☐ Ensure your images are not too big
Run your images through the online platform (https://tinypng.com) to reduce file size.

☐ Check your blogs compatibility across all browsers
Check the main browsers including Edge, Chrome, Firefox, Safari and Opera.

☐ Test your blog display correctly on a range of different devices
You can use online platforms to emulate devices, however these are not always reliable.

☐ Install Google Analytics tracking code
This will allow you to track the amount of visitors to your blog.

☐ Proofread and proofread some more
Review every page on your site, check grammar and spelling.

☐ 404 page works correctly
Test your 404 page by going to /404.php make sure visitors can easily navigate back to the home page.

☐ Test your contact form
Are emails being sent to the correct address?

☐ Upgrade all plugins, themes and WordPress
Ensure your blog is completely up to date to prevent any security issues.

☐ Check all links are working
Go through all posts and pages to check that there are no broken links.

☐ Add alt tags to all of your images
Assigning alt tag names to your images can help with your site's SEO.

☐ Ensure all pages have unique meta data
Using the Yoast SEO plugin, tailor specific meta data for each page and post.

☐ Validate your blog
Use W3C online validators to check your blog is to coding standards.

☐ Ensure your blog loads in under 3 secs
Run your site through an online speed test (https://tools.pingdom. com/).

☐ Set Favicon
A favicon should be 16 x 16px.

☐ Untick "discourage search engines from indexing"
Untick to allow search engines to start indexing your blog.

MAINTAINING CHECKLIST

☐ Empty Spam contents
You can quickly bulk delete all those spam contents.

☐ Reply to comments
Keep people engaged plus it's only polite to reply to a messages.

☐ Monitor Stats using Analytics
Continue to monitor your website traffic using Google Analytics.

☐ Review local search visibility through tools such as Google Search Console
Monitor how well your site is being indexed and that it has no major errors.

☐ Check broken links
Pages might be deleted or archived so check links are still working correctly.

☐ Carry out Security checks
Update your password every few months.

☐ Update WordPress, themes and plugins
Maintain all upgrades to keep your site safe and secure.

☐ Join similar forums
Meet and chat to new people and offer advice. Don't spam forums with links to your blog.

☐ Improve your writing
Try and write 500 words every day to improve your writing.

☐ **Continually review on what could be improved**

Once a week research new ideas and what you could do to improve your blog.

☐ **Compile and send regular newsletters**

Generate more sales with regular newsletter promotions.

☐ **Take regular backups**

Important! Take daily backups so you can be up and running should your blog be taken offline.

☐ **Improve SEO**

Continually carry out keyword research and how you can improve your search engine ranking.

☐ **Reach out to other bloggers**

Ask other bloggers to guest post.

☐ **Keep generating new ideas and being creative**

Look for inspiration from other blogs and websites such as Pinterest.

☐ **Continue to post great content**

Checkout your industry for the latest news.

USEFUL INFORMATION

Blogging platforms

Wordpress.com
www.wordpress.com

WordPress.org
www.wordpress.org

Joomla
www.joomla.org

Drupal
www.drupal.org

Wix
www.wix.com

Squarespace
www.squarespace.com

Blogger
www.blogger.com

Tumblr
www.tumblr.com

Medium
www.medium.com

Selected hosting companies

InMotion
www.inmotionhosting.com

1&1
www.1and1.com

GoDaddy
www.godaddy.com

HostGator
www.hostgator.com

Bluehost
www.bluehost.com

Documentation

WordPress Documentation
https://codex.wordpress.org/

WordPress Directories
www.wordpress.org/plugins/
www.wordpress.org/themes/

Blogging Communities

Triberr
www.triberr.com

Medium
www.medium.com

IndiBlogger
www.indiblogger.in

Inbound.org
www.inbound.org

Kinkk
www.klinkk.com

Google+ Communities
https://plus.google.com/communities